Long Division

The Tupelo Masters Series

Also available as a Tupelo Press audio book on compact disc.

LONG
DIVISION

Poems

Alan

Michael

Parker

T|P

TUPELO PRESS
NORTH ADAMS, MASSACHUSETTS

Long Division.
Copyright 2012 Alan Michael Parker. All rights reserved.

Library of Congress Cataloging-in-Publication Data

Parker, Alan Michael, 1961-
  Long division : poems / Alan Michael Parker. — 1st paperback ed.
    p. cm. — (The Tupelo Masters series)
  ISBN 978-1-932 195-42-2 (pbk. : alk. paper)
  I. Title.
  PS3566.A674738L56 2012
  811'.54--dc23
                    2012011384

Cover and text designed by Bill Kuch, WK Graphic Design.
Cover art: "Post-Dogmatist Painting #288" by Cecil Touchon (http://cecil.
touchon.com/). Used with permission of the artist.

The epigraph is from page 53 of William Carlos Williams's *Spring and All*
(New York: New Directions, 2011), "Pearls" series facsimile edition.

First paperback edition: June 2012.

Tupelo Press
P.O. Box 1767
243 Union Street, Eclipse Mill, Loft 305
North Adams, Massachusetts 01247
Telephone: (413) 664–9611 / Fax: (413) 664–9711
editor@tupelopress.org / www.tupelopress.org

Tupelo Press is an award-winning independent literary press that publishes
fine fiction, nonfiction, and poetry in books that are a joy to hold as
well as read. Tupelo Press is a registered 501(c)3 non-profit organization,
and we rely on public support to carry out our mission of publishing
extraordinary work that may be outside the realm of large commercial
publishers. Financial donations are welcome and are tax deductible.

NATIONAL
ENDOWMENT
FOR THE ARTS

Supported in part by an award from the
National Endowment for the Arts

for Daniel, Ellen, Jesse
& Emma

Contents

The imagination is a —

William Carlos Williams

Long Division

A Christmas Letter

We're never sure anymore.
We redecorate the living room

in a natural theme—grasses in pots,
a cherry veneer, greens and reds—

while in the meadow a zoomburb grows.
The sky tops up; the birds

are strung like dirty pearls.
We're never holier than this:

cutting through the park-like park
on the drive to the office, choosing to be late,

the park-like park cutting through the city,
the city cutting through geology.

And all day the music's in our heads
and planes narrate the weather.

We never know what to feel.
We go to the gym to go

to the beach, where erosion rules.
We reward ourselves with a movie.

Our food glistens in plastic,
kind of like our bodies.

Who can be alone?
This year, so many people died,

and last year, and more next year:
we're unable to be surprised.

Ah, ye gods. I write to you
from prison, surrounded by your flowers.

Thank you all. In the months ahead
let us gather together—to nosh upon

one day as though it were bread and jam.
Cocoa on a snowy afternoon,

or a little wine. Life.
We're all well enough; the dogs get along.

Love—

Family Math

I am more than half the age of my father,
who has lived more than twice as long
as his father, who died at thirty-six.

Once a year for four days
I am two years older than my wife,
until her birthday.

In practical terms I am three times older
than the Internet, twelve times
the age of my obsolescent computer,

five times older than the new century
and only now a half-century old.
I have taught for more than half my life.

Most afternoons of teaching
follow unfinished mornings.
Yesterday I held a book seven times older

than I am. Twenty-eight hours
and a few minutes later, I still recall the smell,
a leathery, mildewed tang.

Seventeen and one-half years ago, my son
was born, which took twelve hours.
His delivery came two weeks late.

The smell in the delivery room
seemed primordial, iron in the blood,
and shit, and another kind of smell—

more abstract, if that's possible.
Twenty-six years ago I studied
abstract ideas in school, and I still don't know

what's possible. Now I teach.
My mother taught for twenty-nine years
until she retired to read.

My friend remembers all he reads—
so when does he finish a book?
I can't remember when I stopped counting

on my fingers: where was I in language?
I feel older than all the wars going on,
but I'm not; some are very old.

Sadness remains the source of my politics.
In my home, very few items I own
are older than I am, and almost none I use.

We say, "the wind dies down."
Is that what we mean? The wind has lived?
When babies are born, they don't know

either night or day. We teach them.
Tomorrow is not my birthday
but all the math will change again.

More to busy me, more to figure and record.
More to have. More to let go.

A Fable for Our Anniversary

You asked to be surprised, so I
traded our last sack of rice
for a little knife curved into a smile,

the knife for a bit of cloth
embroidered by a prisoner,
the cloth for a monkey who was never nice,

the monkey for a bowl of sayings,
the sayings for a pair of silver candlesticks,
the candlesticks for a goose.

The goose bit the dog in the courtyard,
so I traded the goose for a pink bonnet
that makes the wearer invisible.

Who would want to be invisible?
I traded the bonnet for a sheaf of wheat
that shone in the garden for a little while

like a giant piece of golden jewelry,
the wheat for a desk, solid as a bad idea,
the desk for a couple of tickets to a show.

Love, we could go to the show, but the show would end.
I traded the show tickets
for an old trousseau, its linens flush with lavender,

because I knew a man who
would give me a magic goat
for the smells kept between those sheets.

But first the man made me fetch
a cup of coffee from the deli, which I did,
cream, no sugar, an epic quest.

It was one of those dawns that didn't
and then was. The crows were calling
in their office across the street,

all that old business of the soul and such,
but don't you worry, I wasn't scared.
And now I have a goat:

I lead him home, pat his head
and say the words I'm supposed to say—
careful, those words are powerful—

until the goat begins to float into the air,
bleating a bit, and huffing
outside our bedroom window.

Wake up, sweetie!
We've been married for twenty-five years!
I brought you a magic, floating goat!

Eighteen Ways to Consider a Neighbor Whose Holiday Lights Stay Up All Year

1. He's hopeful.
2. He's negligent, and unable to read social cues.
3. This is how he treats his body.
4. He's secretly against mirth.
5. He's obsessed with Immanuel Kant's *The Critique of Pure Reason* (1781).
6. He is spelling something into space.
7. At breakfast he began to the hear the voice of his long-dead, hypochondriac mother saying *Eat! Eat!* and then he felt as though slapped suddenly on the back of the head by the air.
8. He knows my father-in-law, and they've conferred.
9. *Now* is the winter of my discontent.
10. He and the mailman and the UPS woman (she's new) and the Jehovah's Witnesses dressed like busboys and the Trick-or-Treaters and the meter guy with his can of mace and the middle-of-the-night flat *whap* of the newspaper on the front walk. Who can go anywhere?
11. He's helping me be Jewish.
12. When in Rome, burn.
13. How am I to write a poem for fun?
14. He knows. He never forgets.
15. Like lamps lit for all those husbands lost at sea.
16. *Shhhhh.*
17. He's my muse, my indignity.
18. I, with my little words that always go out.

The Take-out Menus in the Lobby

The take-out menus in the lobby are so sleepy,
they are so sore, they have swum oceans,

they have biked cross-town,
they are so surprised, what are they doing here,

what is this place, where are they now.
Sprawled upon the marble, a village,

a diaspora of take-out menus in the lobby
forgotten by the Super in the military light.

When the doors spin and the wind blows in,
the take-out menus in the lobby lift and settle

softly as a sigh, astonished as the moon.
In the fall, swept up. In the winter,

the take-out menus in the lobby
huddle together near the steam,

the pipes banging like a cancer.
In the spring, mud in the gutter

and then jonquils on the sill;
in the summer, curled tight as a whisper.

There go the strollers and the ambulances;
here come the strollers and the ambulances.

There go the strollers and the ambulances;
here come the strollers and the ambulances.

The take-out menus in the lobby
live too many lives at once,

they are so patient, they are so tired,
they are well acquainted with frailty.

There go the strollers and the ambulances.
Here come the strollers and the ambulances.

A Fable for the Persistence of a Dream

He's sure of something, that one-eyed tom,
trotting across the grass,
mugging in the muggy dawn
with the braggadocio of a bigger cat.

Under his missing eye, a new gash—
a blind side turned to meet a raking scratch.
He's wheezing as he wends across
the dewy lawn, rheumy

as the end of a season.
He's probably bloated from the night
spent in the neighbor's garbage,
plundering that Tut's tomb.

What bade him choose?
Sometime in his pissing and ululating
circumnavigation
of my house, he decided

to climb here, into raspy sleep,
to make my bed his haven.
I pet him once, that's all.
Thus instructed, tag team, it's my turn:

teeth minty, nails pointy,
I go to work, to the 27th floor,
to keen all day—

What has become of us?

How shall we know? Where has it gone?
Love, come home—
at the useless moon, the stupendous moon,
the vagabond, bewildering, unfaithful moon.

Night Bus in Vegas

Good hand in his pocket, clinking coins,
the janitor with a shirt named *Hank*
flumps into a window seat,

hip-hop muffled in his earbuds,
the backbeat big enough
to feel. The driver's listening

but not to him,
leaning into her left ear
as she munches cheese-and-lettuce on a roll

right-handed. The bus at night
is a place in space with different rules,
or a river in a river

where music
swallows what it pours.
No one makes a sound attached to anything—

not the four shift workers
aching into their seats,
not the siren passing us by,

rushing to a headline.
Even when an elderly man
with a dotted bandage on his forehead

sighs, he could mean anything.
We're free, we're apart,
we're exhausted and awake,

lit up by the lights too bright
for sleeping, too dim for reading,
lights attached to nothing too.

We're panicked, we're pure,
we're children in the back
of our own memories,

the houses and storefronts flashing by like years;
we're inching forward in our seats,
craning to see what's next,

life arriving,
eager to fall into
the open arms of anybody home.

A Fable, Upside-Down

I see it! he cried and he handed up
a pen, a squeaky toy, and the porcelain chicken
egg cup that Grandma favored.
Stay there, said his father.
What else, said his mother.

He liked living upside-down, the breeze
felt open, gravity was new again,
the sun played him like a tuning fork.
He knew the dew, spent more time with the rain,
saw what the cat would kill.
He liked the math: 4 tires = 1 car.
And: the sine of a driveway = the cosine
of the corner + his sister's bike.
Always, he found what had been
missing for years.

A yogi visited. The upside-down man said,
I am you, and the yogi tapped his foot, yes.
A politician visited. The upside-down man knew
where she had come from, what she used to be.
Go back to your beliefs, he said. *Climb down.*
A doctor visited. The upside-down man asked,
Will all this tingling kill me?

Maybe he was lonely—there were leaves
and sticks
and worms at night.

In time the future made sense to him,
for he knew each ending was the same.

He cherished the rolling nectarine,
the chit-chat palace of the mice,
the good aim of the newspaper girl.
He learned to live with the surf in his head,
the hematological tide, so much thunder.
He knew love's ankle.
When he died, he was buried.
He grew like that: roots, trunk, splashy silver leaves.

Twenty-Two Reasons to Return to the Store

1. Ah, love. What do you need that I have forgotten?
2. The dance of the cashier, the Matisse she hides all day in her clothes.
3. I make lists, lists make me. A list is a foray into the problem of time.
4. I looked for Eurydice in every aisle.
5. "Clean-up in Produce." Guilt.
6. Colors are the forms of desire.
7. Ah, the tumbling life in a wisp of hair that won't stay pinned. All I don't know of everyone.
8. Nothing I am persists. A list stops but never ends.
9. Have you ever considered the supermarket to be like your head? Note the congruities. Not that I trust allegory.
10. What would Rodion Romanovich Raskolnikov do?
11. To resist nostalgia, to live new. To push one's cart out into the lot, climb on the back, and ride.
12. I make it a habit to buy one item each trip that I will not use for months, if ever. In this way, I protest my mortality.
13. She offers the white bird of my receipt.
14. Pay, owe, need, borrow, pay, owe, need, borrow . . .
15. Freud writes, "there is always the possibility that even our painful and terrifying dreams may, upon interpretation, prove to be wish fulfillments."
16. She thanks me for bagging. No one at work thanks me. Poems never thank me.
17. Against chaos.
18. Is a wrong decision better than a dearly held regret?
19. The sculptural problem of bagging, the new challenge each time of new materials.
20. "Gather ye rosebuds while ye may."

21. Ah, love. Too much credit.

22. Receiving my change and receipt and coupons. Her fingers touch mine.

Left Behind

I like the dead who never leave, the ones
still in the room—like Uncle Phil,

who's bound to smack the back of my head again
once we're alone, his response to my pierced ear

thirty years ago. Maybe he was drunk,
or his own dead mom was in the room

smacking him in the head. *Smack!*

Once when my son was young

I drove off without him,
leaving the big boy who had gone to pee.

Nine blocks away, I found myself
talking to an empty car seat.

I was dead, of shame.
It was what death will be,

where no one will see me
u-turning always, across three lanes of traffic.

My New American Lawn

1.
It was too early one morning in
the life of the mind

and I was trying to dial up
a little song in my body

about the wet grass
and the dog padding through
the crunchy, crispy, breakable
blades crackling under paw,

a little song about where she was going
and the carnage of American fescue
left behind in a hopscotch of dogprints
(O careless Love),

the broken tips of the frosted blades
bent so close to the ground;

and a pure feeling was all I wanted
but what I came to understand instead
is nearness, and how the nearest
nearness is just as far as far away.

It's a little like saying I love you
in response to someone saying
I love you.
You see, it's not the same.

The dog gave up her romp
to roll in the grass,
upon some smell in the frosty
pure feeling of the frosty grass.

2.
Let us now blame famous men
for my new American lawn,

men like Frederick Law Olmsted
or Robert Moses, or let us blame
football once again,

or excoriate television
(I love television)
for the year-round daydreams

we exercise as acts of competition.
I blame me, for it's true
what I want to believe

about ryegrass or zoysia or thermal blue
isn't what I feel,
my own anxiety of the idyll,

or so they say. And who are they?
They're the guys with better lawns,
the men who are better men;

the men who are always first
to say with their lawns I love you.

3.

Chemical delight! Weekend cocktails!
And the disease-resistant,
eugenically bred tuff turf
fertilized in the *la-la-la-*
la-bor-a-tory.

Which brings to mind the story
of the man who painted
his stoop and driveway green
and couldn't stop,

the street, the intersection, green;
green, the parking lot of the shopping mall,
green, the windows of the stores.
Then he entered into myth, and green

was the sky, and the birds flew
into the hard green glass
and fell
upon the lawns.

And it was a plague upon
the new Pharaohs.
And it is.

4.

Or maybe I'm thinking about men,
about that chuck of the chin
I chuck to Tim, my neighbor,
when we take out our separated trash,

the way we eyeball each other's
faggot of thinned branches

and bags of mysterious trimmings,
the auguries we read in the forms of leaves,
all of our donations, our prostrations,
our frustrations, our Saturday *do-si-dos*,

the accounts we keep
of each other's clippings,
the oilings of our gears,
the shreddings of our manly lives,

what we throw away and what we pay
other men to deliver, or to take away.

I love you, Tim.
Your lawn is so green, your garbage so clean.

5.
My new American lawn

spreads before me like a centerfold,
pages 16 and 17 of the *TV Guide.*

6.
And with my eyes closed
I can see the worms chewing themselves silly

as the tractors everywhere rev in their garages
(my heart, my heart)
and the newspapers fly,
and the mailboxes salute,

and the sprinklers tuck their little heads
into their little military flowers
for another day of sleep,

and the dogs trot out to do their biz
and the fescue grows so quietly;

and I lie back upon the green grass
as though the new American lawn
were sky

and flap my arms and legs
(where shall I fly?)
(what shall I buy?)

Et in Arcadia Ego

Once there was a car. Once there was a car that had no gas. Once there was a car that had no tires. Once there was a car that stood on blocks in a field of lemony hay and early wild strawberries and shale. Once there was a car that had no gas, no tires, and stood on blocks in a field of lemony hay and early wild strawberries and shale.

Once a parliament of mice lived in a car, a tiny racket. Once a raccoon chewed into a car's oily headrest. Once a porcupine curled around a car's savory gas line.

Once a car was loved by a long road. Once a car read physics to the wind. Once a car bumped to sex. Once a car sung to the radio. Once a car was a weekend.

Once a T-shirt was tied to the antenna of a car. Once rocks were smashed through the left side windows of a car. Once a T-shirt was tied to the antenna and rocks were smashed through the left side windows of a car that stood on blocks in a field of lemony hay and early wild strawberries and shale.

Once a car outlived being a car. Nothing burned. The bushes returned because. The rocks looked the same. Once three deer stood next to a car, helpless as seraphim.

Once a car stood on blocks in a field of lemony hay and early wild strawberries and shale—so open to the sun there was nothing more to open. Once the morning said good morning every day to a car that stood on blocks in a field of lemony hay and early wild strawberries and shale.

Once the deer ate the strawberries, in the natural light of reason. Three deer bounding through the lemony hay.

Bird

I have been losing a battle with a bird
every morning, although the battle
is with myself, so say my 27 therapists, the bird a reminder
sent by whatever I don't believe
to remember what I keep forgetting
because I wake up so damn early, 5:30

every morning, when my battle
feels an unfinished reminder
that I understand less than I believe.
This morning, I thought to fool the bird into forgetting
and so last night I put on my giant bird suit at 5:30,
giddy as a commuter swimming in a huge martini, like a bird

ga-ga over Spring. The sky felt lighter: I had to remember
not to fly, to be a believer
but not a fool—consider Icarus—and never to forget
my basic humanity. But all night until 5:30,
at times awake, I was a bird.
All night the worms were huge, every battle

a belief
in living more. If you're a bird, you never forget
what eating means, and if you're a worm, 5:30
after a little rain means waking into hell, the bird
supping and you're the sup. But I wasn't battling
myself for once, or misremembering

my obligations—although I did try to nest in bed, forgetting
my wife, that was awkward—until just before 5:30
I rose to meet the bird
bird to bird, a Battle

Royale. I chanted to remind
myself of the huge advantage I had in size, a belief

in Nature's equanimity. At 5:30,
then, we met in the wet grass, the bird
a nondescript robin, not a warrior, not the battle
I expected. What did I expect? A reminder
suitable for my forgetting every morning, for my belief
the dawn was singing to make me forget.

I have not forgotten. The ill-fitting bird suit
wears like a belief, a reminder at 5:30
of my humanity, in the battle for my dreams.

Mi Amiga, Cindy

I'm bored as a walnut, Cindy.
I'm tone-deaf as a sunrise.
I'm ready to raise the Level of Difficulty to 1.

The stuff in the back of the fridge—that's me.
The fish in my brain bump against the glass.
Cindy, if I were a suitcase·

I'd need a ribbon on the handle
to recognize myself at Baggage Claim.
I'm a three-legged bed, Cindy;

I'm a toaster that won't give up the toast.
I'm fun as toilet paper, Cindy.
I think like a hammer looking for a nail.

I'm a hole in a teabag, Cindy;
there goes the English Breakfast.
I'm like ink on the back of my knee—

how did I get there?
Cindy, I'm the wrong voltage.
Cindy, I've had to make you up

just to have company.
My parents are nice, Cindy.
I like to bake and when I do

I like to drink and when I drink
I gorge on baked goods
like a hyena with a sack of kittens.

I keep a garden, Cindy,
where I dig deep holes
to idealize the work of real people.

I threw away the asters that you gave me,
Cindy, tossed the blossoms
into the trough in the Men's Room

at the ballpark. Both teams lost.
My name is wrong, Cindy—
everyone calls me Michael.

It's like me calling you Cindy, Cindy.
I'm happy as a Tom Collins,
which means not for long.

Cindy, I'm asleep, I'm awake, etc.
Cindy, where could you be?
Cindy, without you I . . .

Little Lunchtime Fable

When she complained about the lettuce
not on the BLT
and the waiter tripped
and dumped iced coffee on her white linen skirt
and the manager apologized by starting to cry
and blew his big nose into a little handkerchief
that seemed to flutter and float
and stay in the air
like a weird cloud,
she knew that in this moment
by holding still
she would have her three wishes:
Compassion. Fairness. Wealth.

With her eyes closed, last night's moon waxed
and the surf curled
and the moon and the surf together
were here again inside her,

and the wind
was tomorrow's wind, and her eyes
were their original seashells.

She knew the tide carried
the pebble
of her future daughter dancing
on the eve of her tenth birthday
with so many bracelets.

She knew where to find
the young girl who was herself,
whom she had walked by
on the boardwalk,
to whom she had nodded.

She knew the sure course
her blood would take in the sand.
She knew that a day
was a wish
and that knowing
was a wish
and that one of her wishes
was really her mother's.

Here, it's okay:
she handed the manager his handkerchief.
All three wishes wished.

Fifteen Ways to Think about Italian Opera

1. Into a pillowcase, place a red-winged blackbird,
    Aristotle's *Poetics*, an angel, and a sprig of broad-leafed
    parsley. Shake well. *Tosca!*

2. I gave up my tickets, I smashed my CDs, I shredded
    my books, I hammered my toys, I threw my clothes
    from the roof in a storm. Maybe now I'll understand.

3. In Follinger, there's a version of the famous story: how
    Puccini stopped to pick up a multicolored piece of
    glass and was almost run down by a runaway hearse.
    The glass sparkled differently when he turned it in
    his hand.

4. The radio looks so underdressed.

5. Music in a time of war: the percussion section leads
    the Overture, and a pharmacist in Row 3, Seat B begins
    to weep.

6. Follinger writes, "The piece of glass in the Maestro's
    hand held the secret to Act IV."

7. I think I see how love or death can make me sing—but
    the arrival of the Colonel on a mule?

8. Italian opera is like a hat: usually fancy, shading the
    eyes, covering the ears. And then there's the notion that
    so much of the body's heat is lost, if one doesn't wear a
    hat in winter.

9. The pharmacist in Row 3 accepts a tissue from Mrs. de
    Valis. Sometimes we ask to "borrow a tissue," but we
    don't mean for its return. How our hopes can flee.

10. I see the hearse and the panicked horses, although
    Follinger is less than expansive on this point. The clank
    of the bridle and the whiteness of the bit, the reins dragging
    like a wedding dress. The rolling eyes, the dust.

11. As though I have been dug in, rummaged in, while I slept. Then sung about.

12. Intermission. The pharmacist from Row 3 sips a seltzer, looks out upon the city. He won't touch the official notice tucked next to his heart.

13. The piece of glass probably saved Puccini, writes Follinger. Seems right to me: how music-drunk the Maestro was, art-stoned, as someone else's hearse thundered by.

14. I never go to the opera: I'm too busy talking to my family in my head.

15. The pharmacist excuses himself from Row 3, goes home. His son's old room is dark, tacked with postcards, the closet lined with uniforms, scenery and costumes. The part of the grieving father tonight will be played by the grieving father.

To the Peasant, Avram

I found you in a painting of a rickety cart
laden with turnips and the occasional potato

and I brought you home by subway
in a dream, thinking somehow

I might free you of the penury
art has damned you to—

to sit together and sip slivovitz
at my kitchen table, lit by a vase of lisianthus.

The bare patches and tears in your shirt
shone like breaks in the clouds

as the night poured into our glasses.
How could I leave you there, at the museum,

a befuddled sentinel
guarding the 18th century?

I imagine you're a little homesick
and maybe your poor horse needs hay.

Here. Kick off your boots,
lie down and rest at last—

the stew on the stove is almost ready.
Here's a blanket, and a pillow or two:

let us find what sleep affords us both
across the fading centuries,

where the poverty of your eternal station
meets the poverty in me.

A Soap Opera

The role of the soap will be played by my mother,
the role of the towel will be played by my father,
the role of the mirror will be played by my brother
dressed in a shirt of fog.

My students will play the role of the shower—
they arrive together and pour over me
only to drain away.
My lover will play the role of the flowers, oh.

The role of the floor will be played by history:
here we are, and here we go.
The role of the door will be played by Samuel Beckett
in a cameo, the in-between door, the patient door.

Shall we work from the script, or make this up?
The camera tracks us from far away.
What shall I do with my hands?
Wardrobe! I call to Death.

The role of my face will be played by the clock.
The role of my chest will be played
by the bottles of pills, the salves and bandages.
When the doorbell rings, the mice will flee

to their secret roles.
The role of my eyes will be played by twin pennies.
The moon will have a walk-on,
lumbering through the curtains.

Yelling at the Television, I Remember

leaving with a clacking of gravel
the rented summer place on Lake Huron in a cloud
of lavender, the fireflies

scribbling above the tall weeds in the near field
and the ice waiting for winter in the deep,

and the doctor and her nurse in their own
little cottage, lovers, with a bad dog
who would bite every car that turned the corner
until a Camaro killed him;

while the rocks at the edge of the water
took their places, and the bass swam still,

as the flies announced as ever the sweetness
of summer things and came upon us
like mourners on the shore,

as the birds insisted the trees could sing;

where the doctor always read a little
Kierkegaard at tea in her Florida room,
milk and sugar, please, and the sacrifice of Isaac,

accompanied by the wheezing of the pudgy,
snuffling, doomed dog;

as the nurse backed into the room
with a cloisonné tray and supermarket scones.

There they are, with all the other dead
on the blue map re-folded so many times it tore;
Dr. Gibbons, surely
that was her name, Dr. Gibbons of London.

Los Turistas

I have seen the end of the world,
driving in a van of friends
along a synaptic road in southern Spain, grinding gears
in my soul,

protected from my life by a camera,
when an astonishment
appeared: a five-kilometer caldera

like a fallen moon,
the whole huge hole suddenly
cut from the edge of the sea below,
half cliff and half forgotten,

my stunned disbelief
a catechism, straight from the teachings
of St. Anyone.
People were swimming down there,

naked German hippies committed to
their parents' missed opportunities;

babies baked in dreams
under makeshift tents;
dogs cooled forever, up to their chests upon the shoals

as the volcanic, time-ground sand
sizzled with erasure. (Sand *is*
time, sand *is* memory.)

I came to
the finale: the land stopped

where the great divot of the long-dead volcano
cupped the tourists
in a splendid bowl of sea foam.

It was all blue and black and yellow
where the end began, that part I expected,

but not the delights of the hippies
stoned in the tide, with their flappy bandanas
and dreads, smelling religiously
even from here, on high,

beach-blanket Botticelli teens
dropping out to the Dead in the Mediterranean
as though they were angels.

Maybe they were angels: I don't know German.
And maybe the great hole,
half in the earth, half in the sea,
was the hole in each of us—maybe it *is*—

the sleeping and dreaming we do
in the other half of our lives,
and what we learn upon waking:

to cavort in the negative space
of all we'll never know,

like this, with what we call belief.

The Biologist from Pennsylvania

The room ran out of chairs, the lecturer had pictures,
the summer air broke the air conditioner.
From where I sat I couldn't see the screen—

only across the room where the geometry
made by my gaze and the hot afternoon
convened upon a woman

leaning into her listening.
I knew her just a little:
like e-mails we had passed each other

in the hall, and so when
from my angle
her dress opened and her nipple

slipped fully into sight, I felt
uncomfortable and happy, one secret
of her body never meant for me.

The biologist from Pennsylvania said *drosophila.*
I knew to look away, out the window
into the awful day, into the sun.

To say I could not look away would be a lie.
I was more than dimly aware
of my body

getting older, of how a body
is a shadow, depending upon the sun:
I move behind myself, or up ahead.

To claim I felt paternal would be a lie.
The biologist from Pennsylvania said *zygote.*
I practiced the word *decency,*

the shape of the word
flat and without feeling, nothing
like my mouth upon her nipple.

Music from a Passing Car

When the house lights come on, always suddenly,
we blink in stunned surprise
not to be the ones
making out on a wide banquette

but returning to our lives, altogether the same
although a little hungrier, and sweatier, and tired.
Or maybe not the same: the long night is spent
as the servers gather spinning empties

from the sticky floor, and the bouncers
prop open the double doors.
We look for our feather boas and our fedoras,
tug lightly on an ear that's lost an earring,

button up again. We aim
ourselves for the all-night taquería
down the street, now that walking
feels like aiming. From the club lot

a sky-blue pimped-out Honda
waits for the light,
all vibration, tinted windows shimmying
with the pounding bass

of a custom audio system, BOSE
speakers mounted in a rack, and a sub-woofer
pneumatic, adamant, and deep.
Music from a passing car:

a mix of sex and vanity driving away too slowly,
and camaraderie, and embarrassment,
and the desire to distort
the body into thunder.

.

Eight Unfinished Elegies

1. To the bird outside the hospital window, I have lost my mother dying.

2. My mother is a window through which I see the sky.

3. The small sounds of the machines keep my mother dying.

4. A bird flew into the glass: don't touch.

5. As though on the window, I bang my body.

6. Machines keep my mother dying: the sky is a machine keeping my mother dying.

7. The machine of the body dying.

8. Fitted in one hand, the body of my mother.

She Had Read That Hiccups Kill

Risen from the depths of her yellow robe,
she wanted to say it was nothing
as she futzed about her condo patio
in the gray mist before work,
watered the potted tomato mostly done.
There was no particular feeling to the first hiccup,
neither shock nor gorge, but a sense of losing already
the next hour to the little blasts
in her chest and esophagus, of trying to
read the paper, then shower and dress and drive.
Her assistant would be early, and that
irritating realtor, the one with the hair.
They'd work through lunch, the table ruined
with take-out boxes, a little white village,
chopsticks clicking like herons.
Soon enough, she'd begin again to apologize
for being ridiculous, the chthonic jerks of silly air
humiliating, keeping pace but out of time,
the realtor laughing sadly.

She'd wait until tomorrow to go to the E.R.,
until the night was lost, her breathing frayed.
A person could die of this—or really, of anything.
A person could die of walking, of sitting around, of too long
a meeting, of not reading her e-mail for three days
before her fiftieth birthday, of wearing
a yellow robe until that's all she wore;
each hiccup like an alarm
she never could turn off in time,
groping around in the darkness of her chest
for the clock she never could find.

Epithalamion Upon a Third Marriage

We have loved others, we confess:

two dogs and a cat and the occasional
weary, beautiful face on the subway,
fresh snapper and guacamole and lime, oh, lime,

e-mail, mail, the phone set to vibrate,
the hum of the printer warming up
with the hope of human contact,

bread rising in the oven while the snow falls slowly,

the past redone to please the present,

drumming on the steering wheel,
the first green shock of Spring, the plumage,
the full-throated river,

the splurge of spurge, wild grasses and all that flying.

When the light came on, the filament sizzled
and then the light went out, and even this we loved.
Everything has been a test, or maybe a lesson—

if we believed in the God of our Fathers.

Once there was an idea spun in the mind like sugar,

and it was love, how to love
one person, and how to undress the world each day
to find one person. Everything was

buttons and zippers and sashes and strings,
all to undo to find you. Everything
was practicing. Once the new, tiny

buds on the maple (seen through
a high window, a little bit from above)
nubbed into the air, and there the cardinals made a nest.

On television every weekend
the cars raced counter-clockwise—
were they unwinding death?

We have loved others, we confess

over toast and jam, in notes not sent,
when finally alone,
our secrets burned upon the grate.

We look to the sky and see the clouds fraying,
and we look back and see ourselves
round-faced in a window

in every childhood home,
in the ship of the house and the porthole
of our lives, what did we know.

How far away that is, regret the only passage.

We confess, we have loved others,

our jobs too tight, our whispered hopes unraveling
as every night we tried again,
rehearsed ourselves for you.

Apologetic Ditty

Never trust a man who says "honestly."
Never trust the words *disaster relief.*
The delphiniums are withering, the CDs
are degrading, a dragonfly has skimmed
to death against the patio glass,
the letters in books stay dark in the dark.
Never trust the woman who says "You mean to say."
Never trust the words *evacuation plan.*

Never trust an unwrapped caramel
or any other metaphor. Or hopelessness.
Although I love you. Never trust
the man who takes too long to say whatever
he has never been able to say in person
and still can't say and takes so long.
Never trust the words *home remedy.*

I was there: where were you?
Never trust the tongue's twist, loneliness,
a low battery, or a barroom hug.
Sure, the cosmos in the garden won't out-live
the season, feathered and filigreed with frost.
Sure, Nature's obsolete.
Never trust death, or whatever's after.
Never trust the man who says "oblivion is . . ."
Never trust the words *Help Center.*

Never trust the phone to tell
your mom to tell your dad to tell
your grandmother to tell you
I called. I called. Really, I called—

just ask your sister. I called and I called.
Never trust desperation as a form of love.

But I love you. I trust you.
We're working on our love.
Never trust a man who says "work with me."
Never trust the words *simple facts.*
Never trust the words *political solution.*

Never trust a skeptic.
Never trust the message to be
what the man felt when he
gave the message to the telephone
and hoped his feelings would be known.
Sure, the telephone is obsolete.
Sure, Nature's undefeated.
Never trust the words a sister copies down,
all I never meant to say.

Sixteen Ways Old People Terrify the Young

1. They have sex with each other.
2. They drive around.
3. They pretend they're thinking. They pretend they're not thinking about dying.
4. The vigor of diving through the waves (through time) or the splash of the body sprinting toward love. What's a sea, if not for swimming.
5. And what about those old people who walk—I don't know—like seventy-nine miles every morning on the beach? Skin cancer! Yo! They're going to die.
6. "Vex not his ghost: O, let him pass! he hates him
    That would upon the rack of this tough world
    Stretch him out longer" (*Lear*, 5.3.315–17).
7. It's a lie: they were never young.
8. Holidays were invented by old people to dress up and pretend they're all presents for young people.
9. The arc of Story graphed upon the axes of Love and Death.
10. They actually invented the computer.
11. Oh, and they wrote the poems.
12. Their whacked-out sense of sound. No guitars or headphones, no cars or guns; just TV commercials on MUTE, telephones, cats, and the sky.
13. It's like grout or glue or maybe gum. Whatever holds those bones together.
14. They like to die.
15. They like to die in big buildings surrounded by other people. Although occasionally, one of them will take off—to die in the woods or at the beach, some place far away—which accounts for the better old people movies.
16. Or they just die, one on the beach, just like today. With only three people there in the winter to see. A body.

Sprezzatura with Two Rabbits

Talking to the two rabbits in the herb garden, I could be Gerald Stern,
the way he talks to everything, my god,
and really Gerald Stern is always singing to everything,
and everything is singing back.

I tell the rabbit on the left her name is Plato,
and the rabbit on the right she'll have to wait for a name
because so many names are just a necessarily lesser quality
of an original thing. I call both rabbits "she."

I describe to the rabbits Gerald Stern's childhood in Pittsburgh,
his Greek roses and his Borscht Belt beauty and his poem about Auden;
predictably, the rabbits don't seem to care about my story,
jittery and motionless in their agitation, while the stiller I have to stand

to keep my audience, the more some muscle in my left arm
starts to twitch like a bad rhyme,
or like a captive princess kicking over the table
in a fable when the witch wants rabbit stew.

But since I killed so many rabbits in a poem in 1996
with a shotgun—my best weapon then, before I learned to
write about my family—I feel too guilty in advance
to kill and skin and cook and eat

a rabbit named Plato or her pal.
Writing poems makes me hungry for what I can't have, sometimes,
which I think Plato probably knew about poetry, but I need to Google it.
FGI, I tell myself all the time, Fucking Google It.

But now one of the rabbits is named Plato and the other is Gerald Stern,
a combo I'm surprised by, although I suspect that
this poem suspected so all along, and named both rabbits
"she" only as a ruse. Hop away, hop, hop,

hop away free, you bunnies: go back to the greatness
of the garden, your fur dusted with sage and thyme, your lives
opening into a warren filled by the mind of God,
with carrot tops, twenty-seven brothers and sisters, and endless sex;

free of the human need to name, or our crude ambitions
to see whatever light we hope to see,
and hop up and down as we shout *the light! the light!*
before we're devoured by mystery.

The Firefighter's Tale

The firefighter went home for ten days, after working for ten days, and he brought his ax home, which was a firefighter no-no.

When he closed one eye, he saw the apartment complex on Tributary, four alarms and one dead. When he closed the other eye, he saw Lexi, the woman who had failed out of firefighter school, which was okay since she had only wanted to have firefighter sex in firefighter positions and didn't want to be a firefighter. Once, she had said to him, "You know, I'm happy."

When he closed both eyes, he saw his mother and father holding hands. Since he had never known his father, the firefighter decided never to close both eyes.

With both eyes open, the firefighter could choose from the remaining dreams in the cut-glass candy dish by the green chair and the rewired brass lamp: The Tulips Dream, The Coffeehouse Ukulele Dream, The Snapping Fish Dream, The Everyone's Smart Dream, The Regular Tent Dream, The Magic Light That Came On Dream, the sequel to The Regular Tent Dream, The Equator Dream, The Laundromat Dream (Jungle Style), The Sex with Morris Dream, The Thug Life Dream, The Dream Within Reality Dream, The Never Leave Dream, The Everyone Leaves Dream.

He put down his ax: this was no way to behave at home. The ax should go in the hall closet. The firefighter touched the hall closet door high up, above his head, and down low, below his knees, before opening the hall closet door.

"Normal people . . ." the firefighter was going to say to himself, but he didn't care for self-loathing.

If the firefighter rolled himself up in the rug, maybe he could invite Lexi for dinner.

Now, when he closed one eye, he saw a green lawn in the rain, and a couple of birds hopping around because it was hopping season.

Being a firefighter is marvelous, he would have said, but I'm no hero.

He lay down on the sofa with his ax. His own firehouse pillow and bed could have been comforting, but he didn't care for illusions.

His firefighter boots kept him dry all night and all day, for ten days. Safer than last time, he dreamed every dream he found in the candy dish, in order.

Years Later

On the street in front of the pharmacy,
as she balanced her dinner in a take-out box
along with her briefcase and a coffee, double-sweet,

her cell phone died.
She shook it: dead.
She stared into all those little mouths.

It was almost the Fourth of July
and up above the brownstones
presumptive Roman Candles flared,

impossible, ephemeral flowers
sizzling, wishing everybody nationhood.
Neither a star nor a soul.

She leaned against a mailbox, tried to remember—
where had she been going?
And then, with her elbows and her shoulder

rather than her hands, she pried open
the mailbox, dumped in the phone.
Voilà! She was complete, surprised

to feel her body so free.
Which reminded her: she understood.
It was like the moment she had

launched a burning paper boat
upon the family's upstate pond
for her father.

A Vision

In a clear vision on a Tuesday in Toronto
I saw my shadow in the window of
Stein's Downtown Trading Company on Spadina
change and fill and prance;
my shadow was a horse.
He had the long, historical face of a horse
and the thunderous chest, and even though I knew
he was just my shadow, I could see
that he was dappled and dun
and willful and imperious and sly.
I wondered if we were going to ride,
and if so, to where, and would I survive.
He was a great beast, and he made me question
had I ever been a great beast
in any part of my life,
and if so, what had happened
to bring me here.
He never let on what he was doing—
just like me, I never let on,
because I don't want anyone to know
that I don't know.
I was hoping he represented
some kind of beginning,
before the light finished:
then the light finished.
I hoisted my red string-bag of oranges
and packets of deep tea
as I watched him slide away, across the glass,
back to the darkness
of which he was purely made.

A Prisoner of Things

If only this novel were trashier:
if only the hour were true.

The goal here is to burn,
says the sun—

or to lose your place, says the wind.
Or to sleep until

the umbrellas go home,
until the waves decide.

The goal here is to sit here,
says the chair.

Where were you?
asks the hero on every page,

he who spent all winter
killing everything—

oh look, the kittens in the dunes
have caught a mouse.

The goal here is to embrace
nothing, says the air.

If you knew what you wanted
how would you be surprised,

says the sunset.
The seagulls fly back to nostalgia.

You only think you know,
says the sand.

Hot sand! says the sand.
Choose me, says the wave.

Fable, with Bench

Once, a bench in a hospital garden was loved by the sun.
The bench knew that the wind
could only remember where it had been, the addled wind;
that the yellow roses had six weeks to live;
that the rain had its own hours, and work to do.
Maybe the bench could be a doctor to the path.

There were confusing days.
The sun didn't always share, and many afternoons
the bench sat too heavy with being.

Once there was a young woman who
sat on the bench and smoked cigarettes,
her name and photo strung around her neck,
dragging her somewhere,
who loved living and dying as one.

Once there was a man who
would lie on the bench
and fold his hands and stare up
because he too would die some day.

Which bench was important:
choosing was important.
The bench and the man would wait together
for the tops of the elms and the tips of the gate
to hand over the sun
lightly, different, warm.

Poem in a Season of Drought

In the darkness of the shed, the rake and the shovel
hang from their necks.

In the house, we clutch our bric-a-brac,
gaze from a high window over
hedgerows clacking in the dry wind,

over scruffy fields, nothing green,
the leaves shredding to confetti,

and beyond, if one looks far enough,
to the inevitable, enviable sea.

Next to the bed, the radio says
that a drought is a war
to be followed by the news and a Russian symphony.
We hear "sympathy."

It's only May, the summer promises
three months more of this dirt and dust
collecting taxes,

the air filling
with our breathing
out and in

as a warm body in a warm room
becomes a nation without borders.

In a season of drought, what is the season?

Blind, the radio plays and plays,
blank, the television looks away.

Nineteen Baby Anteaters in a Japanese Zoo

1. The baby anteater in the Japanese zoo rides atop its mother's back all day. All day, what a day, with the clinging and the clinging.

2. I'm trying not to be envious. I've given up greed, temptation, prurience, perversity. Lying still makes me happy, so I allow myself three lies each weekday, four on Saturday, five on Sunday. I write them down.

3. Some full-grown anteaters eat as many as 35,000 ants per day. What would I have to eat before moonrise, the rough equivalent of 35,000 ants?

4. I'm missing you. I'm writing all the time about missing you. It's true that I could just hang out with you, rather than write all the time about missing you.

5. The sex of the baby anteater won't be known for a month or two. For now, I've taken to calling it "Smash," a name suitable for an alter ego.

6. Marianne Moore, Marianne Moore, Marianne Moore, Marianne Moore.

7. YouTube is my mind.

8. Once upon a time, a baby anteater swallowed too many ants and had to be assisted by its keeper as the mother anteater was restrained. There's a parable here, even if parables always seem so perniciously mythopoeic, so sociological.

9. Another time, the baby anteater hit its head on a low outcrop of faux rock while being carried around by mom. All the people watching said, "Ohhh!" It was like a poetry reading all over the world.

10. Where is the father? Ask King Laius.

11. Of the pangolin, colloquially associated with the anteater although more accurately of the order *Pholidota*, Marianne Moore writes, "Serpentined about / the tree, he draws / away from danger unpugnaciously."

12. <u>A Poem for Marianne Moore</u>
    The baby anteater in the Japanese zoo
    claws the air
    as though it were there.

13. In praise of gravity. In fear of pain. Not the dying but
    the falling.

14. The baby anteater in the Japanese zoo has little arms
    that look like they belong to a little human. By virtue of
    this association, we comfort ourselves.

15. Reading Miss Moore isn't the same as missing you. She
    writes, "A sailboat // was the first machine." I have no
    sailboat for my longing.

16. By April every year, the ants rediscover my kitchen.
    When I squash them, I refuse to feel bad. Refusing
    to feel bad feels bad.

17. I've given up underwear. I've given up forks. I've given
    up singing. I've given up clocks.

18. The baby anteater in the Japanese zoo stared into the
    pixels, blind as I am.

19. Miss Moore! I name the baby anteater, thus! Marianne
    Moore, Marianne Moore!

Poetry, Inc.

Copy and shred, we animals feed the machines
until the coffee cart comes by at 10,
the urn glowing like religion.

Is your password your birthday?
Copy and shred, we make history.

Whatever we imagine we imagine as money:
copy and shred, shred and copy.

Look out the window: beauty.
Now place one hand on the glass.
Now sell what you feel.

Too many words, too many words,
too many words, too many words;

copy and shred, we flirt with ourselves,
we gaze in the mirror and ask for a raise.

Shred and copy, machines, machines;
the music we make is not our own.
Too many words, too many words,

too many words, too many words,
copy and shred, copy and shred,
too many words, too many words.

Down Winding, Cobbled Streets to the Sea

The pastry shop naps in an iron gown,
                           the éclairs in the window
licked clean in the light.
               By the sudden church a gaunt black dog
hunches in his cassock, Father Dog.
     Every balcony wears a hat and a veil,
a flowerpot on the rail,
               and the occasional sad national flag
hangs like a criminal.

Seven steps down, through a tall alley,
          then six stairs cut in stone—
          then right, where the sea slams
on the seashore, and the color drains from the sand.

The cabanas zipped tight as the faces of widows,
                           a chair all elbows and knees
          props on its side, reading the wind.
The boardwalk lies in splinters
as the summer bikes await dismissal

                    where the town meets the sea
on the tip of the tongue,
               and turning around and tumbling
the shells polish their history.

It's all a painting no one would believe,
or words floating free in the mumbling sun—
                    the liquored sun, the glass sky—
where we awaken, ready again
          to salt our laundry on the line,
          our shirts and sheets and underthings
signaling from the deck to another time.

The Sea, Suddenly Again

Falling asleep with the light on and the mystery novel unsolved—
two lovers in a dinghy upon the North Sea,
one dead on impact and the other drowned—
I wake as though in a different year,
bleached and stunned in the half room,
afloat on a dark, drugged tide.

The gunwales in the shadows are lined with gulls
like agitated clergy, the future finding me
wanting—with my one oar in the skyscraping dark
and the effluvia of my body like garbage—

and then the sea, suddenly again
raises a woman to my mouth,
a susurrus of flesh and salt on my tongue,
tangling in her legs and her lips and sex;

and then the sea suddenly again takes her back,
she to drown and me to die on impact
with the light on and the light on,
to sleep, empty as a boat
or a book abandoned on the hooked rug,
fallen open, and torn.

No Boats Today

It's too hot and there isn't any wind and so
I close my eyes
and walk around a lake I imagined
when I was a kid,

where the sere grasses and the curving shore
and the tight surface of the brackish water
flatten in the white sunlight,
taut as a single sheet of paper.

A sign near the dock says, "No Boats Today,"
which makes sense—a boat's too loud
for memory to allow. No boats:
the dock splinters with disuse,

the shiny pilings slickened,
ruined where time has been.
All of this is my job, to wait for a little wind,
for the slightest shiver of a bird's wing.

Or just to squish around barefoot
where there's no shade, no boats today, no oar,
and every bird
is a mockingbird, a hiding bird.

In the stillness deeper in the stillness
cold currents swirl, the fears
of a child who imagined a lake
and a wild-eyed, prehistoric fish

cruising through the gloom,

bulbous and bumpy and spined.
Years don't matter: I slip in
to where the fish thrashes,

where I come from, the silt and muck,
welcomed home to the danger,
drowned in the darkest colors,
in an ancient human terror.

Another Fable for Our Anniversary

My giant carries me over snowy fields
through a small town above the rooftops
and the frosted ruins of rooftop gardens
over laundry stiff on a line

high as the satellite dishes
everyone warm below

along the highway through difficult woods
and downtown where a guy in a blue shirt
stands at a copier on the 27th floor

a man I might have been

and looks out through the tinted glass
into the snow light

which is like the light in a fable.

I give a little wave and wonder
what he sees eye to eye

if everyone can see
I am in love and I am carried
by love

as though on the shoulder of a giant
whose footfalls boom in the quiet snow.

The guy in the blue shirt is struck
by the slow lightning of the copier.

Being in love
as I am
on the shoulder of my giant
in the snow

I wave to everyone rushing to the windows
such excited office workers

until my giant turns
and down the avenue we go—

to a branch on a tall tree
where my giant leaves me so high up
I can only believe in what's below.

I will live here in the air.
Being in love
as I am

I will live here in the air.

Feeding a Poem to a Horse

An apple would be better
bitten down like the moon
to a crunchy nub
scored with greed

His lips flare in the air
from the fence of his teeth
and his tough tail flicks
where the flies stay

A carrot would be better
than these four-legged lines
that flee from me and never meet
any sweet little need

So we both might gallop
wild and away

Notes

A CHRISTMAS LETTER
The term "zoomburb" refers to "A suburb growing even faster than a
boomburb." From *A Field Guide to Sprawl* by Dolores Hayden (New York:
W.W. Norton, 2006).

THE TAKE-OUT MENUS IN THE LOBBY
After a poem by Adam Zagajewski.

TWENTY-TWO REASONS TO RETURN TO THE STORE
"Gather ye rosebuds while ye may" is from Robert Herrick's poem "To
the Virgins, to Make Much of Time," found in *The Norton Anthology of
Poetry, Fifth Edition;* Margaret Ferguson, et alia, editors. (New York: W. W.
Norton, 2004). The quotation from Sigmund Freud may be found in *The
Interpretation of Dreams,* translated by A. A. Brill (Plain Label Books,
third edition, 1911).

MY NEW AMERICAN LAWN
"O careless Love" refers to the Fats Domino song quoted by Robert Lowell
in his poem "Skunk Hour," from *Robert Lowell: Collected Poems* (New
York: Farrar, Straus and Giroux, 2003). Frederick Law Olmsted was
the designer of Central Park in New York City. Among "master builder"
Robert Moses's many projects were the Triborough Bridge, the West Side
Highway, the Bronx–Whitestone Bridge, the Verrazano–Narrows Bridge,
and Jones Beach State Park, all in New York; his system of parkways on
Long Island is widely considered crucial to the origins of suburban life.

ET IN ARCADIA EGO
The poem's title is borrowed from the painting by Nicolas Poussin (1647)
as well as from the poem by W. H. Auden (1965). The phrase, often
attributed to Horace although originally coined by Pope Clement IX,
translates as "Even I am in Arcadia." The "natural light of reason" comes
from René Descartes's unfinished 1619 treatise, *Rules for the Direction of
the Mind* (Indianapolis: Bobbs-Merrill Company, 2000).

MI AMIGA, CINDY
After a poem by Josh Bell.

LITTLE LUNCHTIME FABLE
"The pebble / of her future daughter dancing" refers to a phrase from the
short story "She Pushed Me," by D. H. Edwards. *The
Collected Stories of D. H. Edwards* (Edinburgh: Diehl Press, 1991).

FIFTEEN WAYS TO THINK ABOUT ITALIAN OPERA
The quotation from C. F. Follinger may be found in *Puccini: Maestro of the World* (Toronto: Hanover Books, 1962).

TO THE PEASANT, AVRAM
For Zoran Kuzmanovich.

YELLING AT THE TELEVISION, I REMEMBER
Søren Kierkegaard's meditation upon Abraham and Isaac appears in *Fear and Trembling* (New York: Penguin Classics, 1995), first published in 1843 under the pseudonym "Johannes de silentio," or John the Silent.

SPREZZATURA
Sprezzatura: "Ease of manner, studied carelessness; the appearance of acting or being done without effort; spec. of literary style or performance..." (from the *Oxford English Dictionary*).

FABLE, WITH BENCH
After a poem by Pablo Neruda.

NINTEEN BABY ANTEATERS IN A JAPANESE ZOO
See "The Pangolin" by Marianne Moore, from *The Poems of Marianne Moore*, edited by Grace Schulman (New York: Viking Penguin, 2003).

THE SEA, SUDDENLY AGAIN
After the novel *Devices and Desires* by P. D. James (New York: Vintage, 2004).

Acknowledgments

Some of these poems have previously appeared in the following journals, often in other versions. I am grateful to the editors of these publications.

American Poetry Review	"My New American Lawn"
Columbia	"Eight Unfinished Elegies" and "Feeding a Poem to a Horse"
Connotation Press	"The Sea, Suddenly Again" and "She Had Read That Hiccups Kill"
The Kenyon Review	"Family Math"
Laurel Review	"Another Fable for Our Anniversary" (as "My Giant")
The Louisville Review	"Epithalamion Upon a Third Marriage"
The Mid-American Review	"Fifteen Ways to Think About Italian Opera" and "Nineteen Baby Anteaters in a Japanese Zoo"
The Naugatuck River Review	"Yelling at the Television, I Remember"
Northwest Review	"Music from a Passing Car," "A Soap Opera"
Numéro Cinq	"Sprezzatura with Two Rabbits"
Pleiades	"A Prisoner of Things"
POOL	"Twenty-Two Reasons to Return to the Store"
Salt Hill	"A Christmas Letter," "Eighteen Ways to Consider a Neighbor Whose Holiday Lights Stay Up All Year," and "Night Bus in Vegas" (as "Night Bus")"
The Southeast Review	"*Mi Amiga*, Cindy"
A Smartish Pace	"Down Winding, Cobbled Streets to the Sea"
Subtropics	"A Fable for Our Anniversary"
Tikkun	"Bird"
Western Humanities Review	"Left Behind," "Poem in a Season of Drought," "Poetry, Inc.," and "To the Peasant, Avram"

"A Christmas Letter" appeared on *Poetry Daily*, May 27, 2009.

"A Fable for Our Anniversary" appeared in *Cork Literary Review*, Volume XIV, Brian Turner, United States editor (Tigh Filí, Cork City, Ireland: Bradshaw Books, 2011).

"Another Fable for Our Anniversary" appeared in . . . *and love*, Richard Krawiec, editor (Durham: Jacar Press, 2012).

"Down Winding, Cobbled Streets to the Sea" was a Finalist for the 2008 Erskine J. Poetry Prize from *A Smartish Pace.*

"Family Math" appeared in *Best American Poetry*, 2011, Kevin Young, editor (New York: Scribner, 2011); in *Pushcart Prize XXXVI: Best of the Small Presses*, Bill Henderson, editor (Wainscott: Pushcart Press, 2011); and also in *Boomtown: Explosive Writing from Ten Years of the Queens University of Charlotte M.F.A. Program*, Michael Kobre and Fred Lebron, editors (Winston-Salem: Press 53, 2011).

"Fifteen Ways to Think About Italian Opera" received the 2009 Fineline Prize from *The Mid-American Review.*

"Nineteen Baby Anteaters in a Japanese Zoo" received a 2009 Editor's Choice Award from *The Mid-American Review.*

"To the Peasant, Avram" appeared on *Poetry Daily*, September 5, 2009.

"Yelling at the Television, I Remember" was a finalist in *The Naugatuck River Review*'s 2010 Narrative Poetry contest.

To Jeffrey Levine and Jim Schley at Tupelo Press, *grazie mille.* To Davidson College, the Fundación Valparaiso, the Virginia Center for the Creative Arts, and the Corporation of Yaddo, thank you for the support. With thanks as well to my careful readers: Tony Barnstone, Suzanne Churchill, Bruce Cohen, David Galef, Cynthia Hogue, Katie Peterson, Kevin Prufer, and always, Felicia van Bork.

Other Books from Tupelo Press

See our complete backlist at www.tupelopress.org

15